TENOR SAX

HAL•LEONARD
INSTRUMENTAL
PLAY-ALONG

COLDPLAY

THE CD IS PLAYABLE ON ANY CD PLAYER, AND IS ALSO ENHANCED SO MAC AND PC USERS
CAN ADJUST THE RECORDING TO ANY TEMPO WITHOUT CHANGING THE PITCH!

Cover photo: Peter Neill – ShootTheSound.com

ISBN: 978-1-4768-1834-4

HAL•LEONARD®
CORPORATION
7777 W. BLUEMOUND RD. P.O. BOX 13819 MILWAUKEE, WI 53213

Visit Hal Leonard Online at
www.halleonard.com

CONTENTS

CLOCKS

TENOR SAX

Words and Music by GUY BERRYMAN,
JON BUCKLAND, WILL CHAMPION
and CHRIS MARTIN

Moderately

IN MY PLACE

TENOR SAX

Words and Music by GUY BERRYMAN,
JON BUCKLAND, WILL CHAMPION
and CHRIS MARTIN

EVERY TEARDROP IS A WATERFALL

5/6

TENOR SAX

Words and Music by GUY BERRYMAN,
JON BUCKLAND, WILL CHAMPION, CHRIS MARTIN,
PETER ALLEN, ADRIENNE ANDERSON and BRIAN ENO

FIX YOU

7/8

TENOR SAX

Words and Music by GUY BERRYMAN,
JON BUCKLAND, WILL CHAMPION
and CHRIS MARTIN

LOST!

TENOR SAX

Words and Music by GUY BERRYMAN,
JON BUCKLAND, WILL CHAMPION
and CHRIS MARTIN

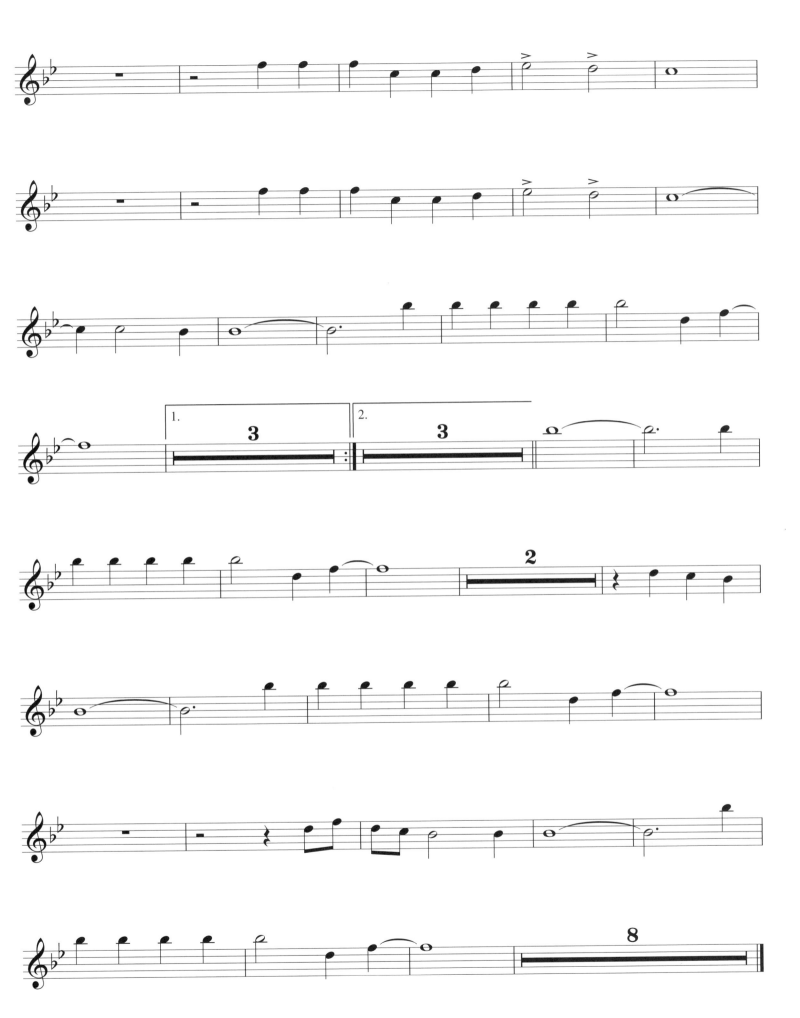

PARADISE

TENOR SAX

Words and Music by GUY BERRYMAN,
JON BUCKLAND, WILL CHAMPION,
CHRIS MARTIN and BRIAN ENO

System off

THE SCIENTIST

TENOR SAX

Words and Music by GUY BERRYMAN,
JON BUCKLAND, WILL CHAMPION
and CHRIS MARTIN

15

SPEED OF SOUND

TENOR SAX

Words and Music by GUY BERRYMAN,
JON BUCKLAND, WILL CHAMPION
and CHRIS MARTIN

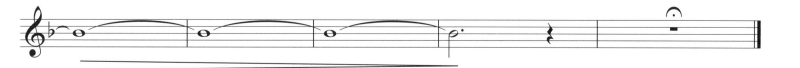

TROUBLE

17/18

TENOR SAX

Words and Music by GUY BERRYMAN,
JON BUCKLAND, WILL CHAMPION
and CHRIS MARTIN

VIOLET HILL

19/20

TENOR SAX

Words and Music by GUY BERRYMAN,
JON BUCKLAND, WILL CHAMPION
and CHRIS MARTIN

YELLOW

21/22

TENOR SAX

Words and Music by GUY BERRYMAN,
JON BUCKLAND, WILL CHAMPION
and CHRIS MARTIN

VIVA LA VIDA

TENOR SAX

Words and Music by GUY BERRYMAN,
JON BUCKLAND, WILL CHAMPION
and CHRIS MARTIN